About this book

How many of us know about religions of the world other than ours? Do we ever wonder why some of our friends have different beliefs from our own. We have all seen the beautiful saris that many Indian women wear, but have we ever wondered what customs and beliefs our Hindu friends might have? In this book Partha and Swasti Mitter trace the development of the Hindu religion from its origins 5000 years ago on the banks of the River Sindhu to the Hare Krishna people who can be seen wandering the streets of London and other cities preaching their message of peace and tolerance.

The book is illustrated with forty-six black-and-white photographs and there is a glossary, a further reading list, and an index.

Hindus
and
Hinduism

Partha and Swasti Mitter

Other books in this series

Buddhists and Buddhism
Christians and Christianity
Jews and Judaism
Moslems and Islam
Sikhs and Sikhism

First published in 1982 by
Wayland Publishers Limited
49 Lansdowne Place, Hove
East Sussex BN3 1HF, England

© Copyright 1982 Wayland Publishers Limited

ISBN 0 85340 908 0

Printed and bound in Great Britain by
R. J. Acford, Industrial Estate, Chichester, Sussex.

Contents

1 Who are the Hindus?

The Hindus are the people who originally settled in India over 5000 years ago and Hinduism was their religion. But Hinduism is also found in South-East Asia, and today some Europeans believe in Hinduism as well.

The word Hindu is not Indian. It was given by ancient Persians to people living on the banks of the River Sindhu in Panjab. Because the Persian language did not have the sound for 's', they pronounced the word as 'Hindu'. Later, Greeks and Romans changed it to Indika, which we in turn have changed to India. Thus Hindus were the people who followed the religion of ancient India, one of the oldest of the world's religions. Ancient Hindus, however, did not call themselves by that name; they knew their religion as 'the eternal religion' (Sanatan Dharma).

Can you tell Hindus by their dress? Yes, to some extent. Men wear a piece of white cloth, which is called a dhoti, and women wear the sari, which is a very long piece of cloth which they wind around their bodies. The brahmin priest is recognized by his sacred thread. But Hindus also adopted Middle Eastern tunic and trousers under Moslem rule. Today most Hindu men have taken to European clothes as being more practical, though women have not given up wearing the sari.

Do Hindus observe special food restrictions? A Hindu will not eat beef, because the cow is held in affection and is sacred to him. Most Hindus are vegetarians, because they respect all living creatures. They also maintain strict rules about cleanliness and where and with whom they eat. Today an increasing number of Hindus do not accept these restrictions.

*Pilgrims come from many
parts of the world to
bathe in the river Ganges.*

Do they speak a special language? Hindus speak the language of the region to which they belong but they all regard Sanskrit, the language of their religious books, as sacred.

Hindus all believe in rebirth after death, or reincarnation. Because a Hindu accepts the unity of all life, he believes that human beings can be reborn as animals if they are not good in this life. Similarly, animals have a chance to better themselves in the next life. Because of this belief Hindus always treat animals with kindness because they might possibly be reborn as one's friend or relation.

Ancient Hindus also believed that Hindu society could be

Left *The cow is a sacred animal to the Hindus and they will not harm one. Often the people feed a cow although they have little food to spare.*

Right *The sari is the national dress for most Indian women. They are usually made from brightly-coloured silk or cotton.*

divided into four classes – priests, rulers, traders and peasants. A person's position in life was therefore decided by being born into one of these four groups in society. This unpleasant restriction was called the caste system by Western societies. Today, although many Hindus ignore these restrictions, they still remain strong in some areas. The caste system also discourages foreigners from becoming Hindus because it states that you have to be born a Hindu. Despite these restrictions, there are many cases from ancient times of foreigners being accepted as Hindus. Although Hindus were unwilling to admit foreigners into their own religion, they were prepared to admit that other religions were equally true, and that everyone should have the freedom to choose their religion.

Today many Hindus do not follow all these ideas; they probably practise some and reject others. Yet they still call themselves Hindus.

2 The origins of Hinduism

Hinduism has no founder as such, unlike Christianity, Islam or Buddhism. It has developed over the centuries and there were important teachers at each stage of its development. The earliest civilized people in India lived in two great cities, Harappa and Mahenjodaro on the Indus river, some 6000 years ago. They worshipped a mother goddess and a horned god as well as honouring trees and animals. The next people to arrive, in 1500 BC, were called Aryans. Their language was similar to many European langauges. At first the Aryans conquered the earlier settlers, but eventually peace was made and the two races were able to exist side by side. Hinduism, as we call it, developed from the religions of these two groups. It was the Aryans who introduced the caste system.

The most sacred collections of the Aryan's hymns were called the four Vedas – Rig, Sama, Yajur and Atharvan. These were also called Sruti, which means 'heard', as they were held to be directly received from God. To preserve their purity, the Vedas were not written down until recently; instead they were faithfully memorized. For over 3000 years brahmin (priest) children had to learn by heart every single word in the Vedas even if they did not understand the meaning. Because some of the hymns are sung they can also tell us a great deal about ancient music. To a Hindu the Vedas are still the most holy works.

What are these hymns about? Like many primitive people, the Aryans worshipped nature, in particular the gods of the skies – wind, sun, sky and thunder – who were described in the hymns as 'shining objects'. The gods were mostly portrayed as men and warriors, since Aryans themselves were

*This illustration shows
the god Krishna.*

warlike. These Vedic people had a very simple approach to their religion and felt no need to have images or temples for their gods. They did, however, perform sacrifices which involved offering to the gods the food and drink the Aryans themselves were fond of. In exchange, the gods were expected to grant them all the good things in life. The Aryans believed that during the sacrifice the gods descended to eat and drink with them. But the gods did not accept the gifts unless the ritual was properly performed. The Vedic hymns ensured that the sacrifice was performed in the correct way. Though generally Vedic hymns are dry formulas for sacrifice, they also contain many moving poems

Left This picture also shows Krishna, together with his admiring companion Radha.

Below This illustration shows the god Brahma being born. The figure on the left is Kali or Durga.

This picture shows the god Rama with the goddess Sita next to him. At their feet is the monkey-god Hanuman.

about nature, such as the beautiful hymn to the Spirit of the Night.

The Aryans were a simple, happy race who lived in close contact with nature. They do not seem to have given much thought to life after death. They believed that after death, men went on to live in a paradise, which they called The World of the Fathers. But ideas about hell were still undeveloped. The gods themselves were not much better than men and were kept happy with offerings. But the traces of a higher moral idea could be found in one god, Varuna, who could not be bribed by sacrifice. He upheld the law (rita) which governed both human morality and the universe, and was responsible for punishing evil-doers. He was so pure that his followers trembled in his presence and asked for forgiveness for their sins when they addressed him.

3 The sacred books

Aryan society, which was centred on the individual village, developed peacefully for 500 years before Hinduism took a new turn. As large and powerful kingdoms arose, old tribes broke up and tribal loyalties disappeared. People were forced to move into large and impersonal cities. Members within each family were scattered. Life became uncertain and the people felt insecure. This insecurity made them think about this life, and life after death. This period of doubt gave rise to a number of great teachers in India, as it did in China and Greece.

Also at this time two ideas were developing which were later to take firm hold of many Indian religions, including the two major Indian religions of Hinduism and Buddhism. The first idea, called Samsara, taught that the souls of both human beings and animals go through a succession of births. Samsara thus formed a vast chain of life with links from the lowest animals to Man, the highest living being. The second idea, Karma, stated that whether a person was born as a higher or lower creature in the next life was decided by behaviour in the present life. These two ideas, Samsara and Karma, are a central part of Hinduism. Through the idea of Karma, the Aryans attempted to understand the problems of suffering and inequality they found around them. Belief that unhappiness in life was caused by misbehaviour in a past life made people accept their condition more easily. But this also made them endure needless suffering inflicted by others. The prospect of a better next life also gave them the encouragement to lead moral lives, as this

14

In this picture Hanuman is carrying the gods Rama and Lakshmi.

offered them the chance and hope to better themselves. Even though Hindus do not deny that human life is better than animal life, they recognize that animals too have souls.

At about this time yoga, a system which taught how to control the mind by controlling the body, was introduced.

The most important teachings of this period of uncertainty were later collected under the title of the Upanishads. This word means meetings between teachers and pupils. They are also sometimes known as Aranyakas, forest books, because they were composed in the peace and solitude of the forest. Hinduism has no specific founder. We do not even know the names of the early teachers who held intense discussions about the mystery of life and the universe, and the nature of the soul. The essence of their teachings is, however, to be

found in the Upanishads.

In the Upanishads the wise men agreed that death was painful. It was even worse to face many deaths in endless streams of rebirths. They taught that one had to gain true knowledge through meditation and the renunciation of worldly pleasures. What was this true knowledge?

The sages described Brahman as the source of all creation, and of time and space. As vast as the whole universe and more minute than the smallest particle; and yet it was everywhere. They explained this difficult idea with a story:

Shvetaketu's father asked him to fetch a bowl of water and some salt. He then poured the salt in the water and asked Shvetaketu to taste it. 'Can you taste the salt?' he asked. 'Yes,' answered Shvetaketu. 'Can you see the

Left *This Hindu priest is reading from the Bhagavad Gita, the holiest book of the Hindu religion.*

Right *This picture shows the goddess Lakshmi. Many Hindu paintings show this goddess with water lilies in her hand or in the background. Worshippers often put lilies around her statue as well.*

salt?' 'No,' said Shvetaketu. 'My son,' said the father, 'just as you can taste the salt but cannot see it, so Brahman is everywhere and yet is so subtle that the human mind cannot comprehend it. You too are the Universal Essence.'

What is Brahman? The teachers agreed that Brahman was the principle that governed the cycle of rebirths and the universe, but that this principle was beyond most people's understanding. For this reason they asked questions which they thought would help to make the nature of Brahman clear. Some of these teachers spoke of Brahman as a man. This view of Brahman is like the idea of God in Christianity, Islam or Judaism. Others were not satisfied with this answer, for they felt that it reduced Brahman to the level of Man.

The passages which describe the qualities of Brahman in the Upanishads are perhaps the most difficult to understand. Brahman had no beginning, nor an end. It was neither man nor woman. It covered the whole universe in extent and yet it was so tiny that we could not comprehend it. It was completely unmoving and at the same time the source of all energy. All these statements seem confusing and contradictory but they were meant to provide a glimpse of the deepest mysteries of life. Today some scientists believe that these Indian teachers had grasped the idea of molecules, which are the minute particles which make up everything.

The Upanishads also taught that the human soul (Atman) was part of the Universal Essence (Brahman), as told in Shvetaketu's story. The true knowledge was the idea that Man was a part of Brahman and eventually went back to it. Life here on Earth was only a brief stop on our eternal journey. The Upanishads warned against believing in this life as the only one and called it an illusion (Maya). They also said that true knowledge was gained through meditation. When this was gained, death would have no terror.

18

Opposite left *This strange figure is the elephant-god, Ganeshi.*

Opposite right *Vishnu and Lakshmi. Flowers are offered to the gods in the form of garlands which are placed around their statues.*

Right *This is a model of the goddess Durga. It has been made during the festival of Durga Puja. At the end of the festival the image of the goddess will be immersed in the river.*

Because, for these wise men, religion meant the search for knowledge they believed that all religions contained some valuable truth. They used the story of The Elephant and the Blind Men to illustrate this important lesson. Some blind men wished to find out what an elephant looked like. One man touched the elephant's trunk and asserted he knew what the beast looked like. Another touched its tail, the next touched its tusk, and so on. Then they started quarrelling as to what the elephant really looked like, for each of these blind men was confident that he knew the shape of the beast. But in fact each one knew only a part of the elephant.

This part of their religion is very difficult for many Hindus to understand or live by, but it is still a very important part.

4 Bhakti – the devotion to God

The next important development of Hinduism took place in India in the centuries preceding the birth of Christ in the Middle East. The teachings of the Upanishads had failed to satisfy the emotional needs of ordinary people who found the idea of Brahman and Atman too difficult to understand. They needed a god to whom they could relate and turn for spiritual comfort, someone who would lead them towards salvation. To a Hindu salvation meant freedom from the endless cycle of rebirths (Mukti). This new development was called Bhakti, which taught love and devotion to one's chosen personal god. Many religions seek to establish a personal relationship between individuals and a god, who is loved by his followers as they love their dearest ones. In return, they believe their god has the same love for them.

From this period on, most ordinary Hindus had a personal devotion to a god who they believed would look after them after death. This new idea was far more attractive than trusting in the knowledge of the Vedas and Upanishads. Gradually this belief in a personal god overshadowed other beliefs and inspired countless numbers of wandering saints, and hymn-singers who travelled across India singing the praises of their own beloved gods.

Bhakti gave rise to new religious books which related dramatic stories of gods and their victories over evil forces. The ideas of Bhakti also inspired two of the greatest poems in Indian literature, the *Ramayana* and *Mahabharata*. The most popular parts of these books were called the Puranas and celebrated the triumphs of the great gods. Unlike the Vedas, which only the highest caste were allowed to learn, these works belonged to everybody, even the most humble.

This sculpture is of the demon-king, Ravana. He was defeated by Rama.

The greatest book inspired by Bhakti is *The Song of God*, also called *Bhagavad Gita*, composed in the second century after Christ. It is still the most inspiring book to a Hindu. This work was the great modern Indian leader Mahatma Gandhi's constant inspiration during hours of crisis. In this long poem, God takes the form of Krishna, who was a great hero. Krishna reveals to Arjuna, his friend, his true divine form. Arjuna is the only human being who knows Krishna's true identity and he is overcome with terror for he cannot bear God's splendour. Krishna reminds Arjuna of his power but also reassures him of his love and instructs him in the

Above left *This is a shrine to the goddess Durga.*

Above right *This small statue shows the most famous incarnation of Vishnu — Rama.*

true religion. He should respect the Vedas and Upanishads, but for his own salvation Arjuna must trust God totally. Because of Krishna's love and grace for his worshippers, they are spread the uncertainties of Karma and Samsara.

5 The followers of Vishnu and of Shiva

Hinduism today is known for its colourful gods. With the development of personal gods came images and temples dedicated to them. At first the large number of Hindu gods confuses people who are not Hindus. All the different gods, however, can be divided up into two main groups, those belonging to Vishnu's group, and the others being part of Shiva's family. Do Hindus worship all the gods and regard all of them as equally important? Remember the story of The Elephant and Blind Men in the Upanishads? Hindus pay respect to many gods because they were taught that all the gods were simply different aspects of a single being. At the

This statue of the monkey-god has been garlanded with flowers by his followers.

*The god Shiva is pictured
here with Parvati.*

same time every Hindu has their own favourite god on whom
they lavish all their devotion. In almost all cases the choice
is between Vishnu and Shiva. This attitude enabled Hindus
to be tolerant towards other religious groups. The followers
of Vishnu or Shiva have seldom attacked one another solely
for the sake of religion, a fact that has often surprised people
of other religions.

Although a Hindu respects both Shiva and Vishnu, he
may still have his favourite between the two, because the
nature of one god particularly appeals to him. Vishnu is gentle and benevolent, and associated with creation, the sun
and with light in general. He also takes human or animal
form and descends to the earth to save mankind when it is
overwhelmed by the forces of evil. Vishnu's animal and
human forms are called Avatars or Incarnations. Avatars are
meant to remind human beings that Vishnu feels himself

24

close enough to living beings to be born as one. Also if human beings are good enough they can aspire to divinity because a little bit of Vishnu enters into them. Of all the incarnations of Vishnu, the greatest is probably Krishna, the Bhagavad Gita god who appeared as a god on earth. Some time after the Gita was written, Krishna came to be identified by his followers as the god of love. His love for the souls of mortals was unlimited. He is perhaps best explained in the story of Krishna and Radha, the young girl whose love for him knew no bounds.

Those who prefer Shiva look for something different. He is a fierce god who demands absolute allegiance from his worshippers. He rules over death and life, and over both human and natural fertility. He is imagined as time itself, the destroyer and creator of all worldly things. His passion is dancing: he creates life when he dances. He will also dance at the end of time, when the universe will be swallowed up by a raging fire. Hindus believe that creation goes hand in hand with destruction. Because Shiva rules over death his

This amazing sculpture
of the goddess Kali.

*Hindu temples are
carefully looked after.
This picture shows a
shrine to Ganeshi.*

attendants are ghosts and hideous spirits. He is also a great
ascetic who shuns all forms of wealth. Although Shiva has no
hunting incarnations he too takes up arms against forces of evil
whenever this is necessary.

An important part of Shiva's cult is the special respect
paid to the great mother goddess, who is full of love but
does not hesitate to punish wickedness sternly. This goddess is very different from those worshipped by the early
people; they were usually male. The mother goddess is
believed to be as powerful as Shiva himself. Of her many
forms, the most popular are Kali and Durga. As Kali, she
becomes a horrific and ugly woman who rides on a lion and
destroys the evil buffalo demon. While she punishes
wrong-doers mercilessly, she is gentle to her followers and
also towards her companion, Shiva. Shiva and Durga are
regarded as inseparable and their companionship is
regarded by their worshippers as the ideal marriage where
both partners are eternally loyal to each other.

Other gods in Hindu mythology have very little power and following. They are rather more like colourful characters in stories. Some, like Brahma, the grandfather god, or Surya, the sun god, were in the Vedas and continue to figure in rituals. Other popular gods include Lakshmi, the goddess of wealth, and Ganesha, the elephant-headed god, who ensures success in any job or business.

Something that is puzzling in Hinduism is that there are a bewildering number of gods with very many names. How can we make sense of this confusing variety? The Hindu religion is a mixture of many different beliefs because whenever the ancient Hindus came across an unfamiliar god belonging to a different religion, they did not simply reject it. Instead they tried to understand it by looking for features it shared with their own gods. If the new god was gentle and friendly he was compared with Vishnu. If he was mysterious and fierce he was grouped with Shiva's sect. In this way many of the other religions that were popular in India were included in Hinduism.

This family group have come to make an offering to Ganeshi the god of Plenty.

6 Images and temples

By the third century after Christ, Hinduism was well established with many of the features it was to retain until this century. During the early periods the people had not needed images of the gods because sacrifice was the main religious activity. Now many Hindus wanted to have images of Vishnu and Shiva which they could worship. Beautiful images of the many different gods and goddesses were fashioned.

Artists were encouraged to portray the heroic stories of how the great gods had destroyed evil forces and restored goodness on earth. Temples were built to house those images. The rich and the poor in the community contributed towards the cost of building these temples and they took great pride in them. Many of these temples, especially the

This is the city of Benares, one of the holy cities of Hinduism.

Elephants stand guard over this shrine to the gods.

ancient ones, are among the most inspiring pieces of architecture ever built. Sculptures on the walls of the temples told the stories of the gods. These carved stories were meant to help teach the people about Hinduism in an age when only a small number of people were able to read or write.

But when do Hindus visit their temple? Most practising Christians go to church every Sunday, but a Hindu does not lose his religion even if he never visits a temple in his life. He is free to go whenever he likes. He may visit it once a day, once a week, once a month, or once a year. Not all Hindus gather together at a certain time to pray in a temple as Moslems do. The temple is in fact the house where the great god lives like a beloved and honoured guest. Remember how the followers of the Bhakti religion treated their god as a beloved friend? So practising Hindus look after Vishnu or Shiva in the temple as they would their closest relations. They have various ceremonies during the day – the god is awoken at dawn, fed the main meals of the day and then put to bed at night. Looking after the gods is a full-time activity, so each temple employs a priest. Ordinary Hindus do not go to the temple simply to pray; they also go there to 'view' (Darshan) the image of the god in much the same way as they would visit a friend. In the temple they perform 'puja', which means offering fresh flowers and food to the god. This food is then blessed and given back to the worshipper who can eat it knowing he has shared it with his god.

Every family, wherever possible, has its own private chapel for which a room is set aside in the house. Here the household god is kept. It is a very sacred room and is kept

This shrine is dedicated
to the goddess Durga.

Not all Hindu shrines are in large temples. This old man stands in front of his own shrine to the goddess Kali.

scrupulously clean. No one is allowed in with shoes on or in dirty clothes, unlike the public temple which may be visted according to one's inclination. It is here the family pray once in the morning before starting the day and once at night before going to bed. Here too the Bhagavad Gita will be read.

Although a Hindu will regard the god in the temple and in the home as a living god, he knows at the same time that the image is there only to remind him of god. He is careful not to confuse the image with the god. This can be seen in a seasonal festival like Durga Puja. At this time an image of the goddess is made with infinite care by a sculptor. It is then consecrated or blessed by the priest and for four days all the worshippers feel very close to the goddess. When the festival is over the image is thrown into the river. This is to show the worshippers that the statue is really just an image of the goddess.

7 Hindu society and laws

We have seen how Hindus are free to choose their own path to salvation or Mukti (freedom from rebirth). On the other hand, they are also bound by very strict social rules. Hinduism is not simply a matter of faith: it is also a strict set of rules for social behaviour. So the word 'Dharma' in Hinduism, which is perhaps the closest translation of the English word religion, does not only mean belief, but also a strict set of rules for a way of life.

The books on Dharma deal with general moral laws, such as honesty, kindness, hospitality and truthfulness, common to all great religions. All Hindus are expected to follow these. But the books on Dharma also say that all human beings are not born equal, because of their previous lives. They divide the whole community into four great classes (Varna) and give specific duties to each class. The Dharma of the Brahmin (priests) is to preach and to preserve sacred learnings. The second group, Kshatriya, kings and warriors, are born to rule and protect the people. That of the third group, Vaishya (traders), is to increase the wealth of the land. The fourth group, Shudra (peasants), should serve other classes. So the profession of a male child was fixed at birth. He had to enter the family profession and was not allowed to move into a different one. The law held that the moral duty of each class was different and that it was far better to do the duty of one's class badly than to do someone else's well. These laws were strict and oppressive and often they were not followed. There soon appeared many professional classes (called castes in English) which did not easily fit into any of the great classes (Varna). Today there are numerous castes in India.

Until recently a Hindu girl expected her parents to provide her with a dowry.

The law also made strict rules about topics such as marriage and food. Everything in the world was either pure or impure. To preserve the purity of each caste no one was allowed to marry outside their own group or caste. If any food which was to be eaten by a member of a high caste was touched by someone from a lower caste that food became impure. To prevent this, castes were not allowed to eat with other castes. These ideas may have originated in the early period of human history when the magical power of many things, living or otherwise, was deeply feared.

These primitive ideas have had a great influence on Hindu

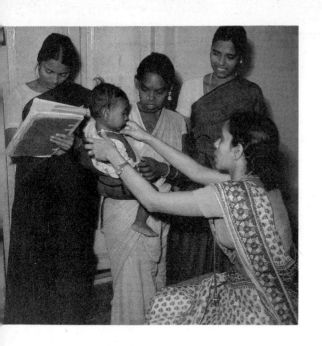

Left *Today more and more Indian women are taking jobs that previously they were not allowed to do.*

Right *The number of women doctors in India is increasing rapidly. Nursing is also a popular career for young girls.*

society. Individual jobs were given to specific castes. For example, a priest (Brahmin) could only belong to the highest caste, while a peasant (Shudra) belonged to a very low one. All the really unpleasant jobs, such as cleaning the streets and lavatories (in those days there was no sanitary flushing system), were performed by one particular caste – these unfortunate people came to be called the Untouchables. Other castes were so worried that even the touch of a sweeper would make upper-caste Hindus impure, that they banned these people from living in the community. They had to live outside villages and towns. Whenever they entered a village or town to do their jobs, drums were sounded to warn other Hindus not to approach them. This prevented them from polluting others even accidentally.

The life of the upper-class Hindu was divided into four stages. A central idea of the Hindu way of life was that it was important for each person to make way for the younger generation, who must also be given a chance. Thus the child

went away to live in his teacher's house to receive education. When he came of age he married, settled down and had children. When the couple grew old they retired from active family life, settling down in a quiet part of the woods to spend their time thinking about God. The last stage, which expected people to lead rather severe lives, was not meant for everyone, but only those who were able to bear quite a lot of hardship.

These rules about class duties during each stage of life formed the basis of the Hindu religion. The total of a Hindu's religious duties is called Varnashramadharma.

At present, these four stages of life are not strictly followed by Hindus, although they offer a model for them to follow. The caste laws have become much weaker. When India became independent in 1947, discrimination on the basis of caste was made illegal. Untouchables and other lower castes are now encouraged to take up jobs which they were formerly prevented from doing.

8 Hinduism and Islam

Hinduism received its first serious challenge from the Islamic religion in the thirteenth century. Moslem rulers from central Asia invaded India and set up an Islamic state. In the process many temples were destroyed. For the first time the Hindus became subjects of rulers who discouraged unrestricted worship of Hindu gods. This made many Hindus even more strict about observing religious and caste rules, whilst large numbers of low-caste Hindus became Moslem. Some Hindu preachers in fact found they had much in common with a particular group of Moslems called the Sufi Mystics. Both these groups were unconventional and sought to reach God directly through love. Some of the great Hindu saints such as Kabir, Tukaram, Tulsidas and Nanak took good things from both religions and their songs moved people of both religions, irrespective of which caste they belonged to. Many Hindus had regarded the caste system as evil even before the arrival of Islam. The great religious leader, Chaitanya (1485–1533), whose personal god was Krishna, welcomed not only people of all castes but Moslems as well. Chaitanya's message of love and brotherhood is carried across the Western world today by the movement known as the Hare Krishna Sect (International Society of Krishna Consciousness).

By the late eighteenth century, when India was brought under British rule, Hindu society had become excessively narrow. Women and low-caste people suffered great hardship and many honest and liberal Hindus felt that, if Hinduism were to continue as a healthy religion, reforms were necessary. Christian missionaries also arrived with the intention of converting Indians to Christianity and immedi-

*The Hindu temples are
often beautifully
decorated with statues
made of precious metals.*

ately pointed out the harmful practices in Hindu society.
The great nineteenth century Indian leader, Ram Mohan Roy
(1772–1833), realized that some people had forgotten the
high principles of Hinduism and were mistakenly worship-
ping idols as the true gods. He supported the Government in
its efforts to ban the caste system and to reform Indian society. Ram Mohan Roy knew many languages, including
Sanskrit, Arabic, Greek, Latin and English. From his read-
ings on books of Christianity and Islam as well as from the
Upanishads he learnt that all these religions spoke the same
truth. In this he was following the age-old Hindu attitude.

He created a reformed Hindu religion which combined the 'Brahman' and 'Atman' of the Upanishads with the Christian idea that all men are born equal in the sight of God.

By the end of the nineteenth century, however, Europeans themselves had discovered the attractive qualities of Hinduism. This fact encouraged the spread of Hinduism amongst the Indians, who had become demoralized after being conquered by the British. Dayananda Saraswati (1824–83) was a powerful reformer and founded a reformed Hindu sect, the Arya Samaj. This sect also denounced the caste system as evil, and called for Hindus to return to the pure religion of the Vedas.

The most popular religious leader of the nineteenth century was probably the saint, Ramakrishna (1834–86), who

Left The 'ghats' at Benares are often crowded with pilgrims waiting to bathe in the river and purify themselves.

Right Indira Gandhi is Prime Minister of India and an example of the high position many Indian women are achieving now.

illustrated the profound truths of his religion with simple and moving stories. In a true Hindu manner he accepted the truth of all religions and accepted many of the lessons of Christianity. He died before he became well known, but through his greatest disciple, Vivekananda (1863–1902), his message was spread not only throughout India but also to many other areas of the world. Vivekananda arrived at the International Congress of Religions in Chicago in 1893 as an unknown monk. After his speech about the nature of Hinduism at the conference, his fame spread throughout America and Europe, and he attracted a large number of disciples. In the West, especially, he convinced many of the greatness of Hinduism. But he was also aware of the grave social injustices from which modern Hinduism suffered. He

Today more Indian children are being educated than ever before.

therefore decided to make it his life's duty to teach Indians to face these evils and to rid Hinduism of them. He was not ashamed to learn from Christianity and felt that Hinduism lacked any organizations like the Christian missionary societies to help people. To fulfil this need he founded the Ramakrishna Mission, named after his teacher. Today the Ramakrishna Mission exists in many major European and American cities. Amongst his numerous disciples was an Irish lady, Margaret Noble, who received the name Sister Nivedita (Dedicated). She continued her master's work after his early death.

The greatest nationalist leader of modern India was Mahatma Gandhi (1869–1948). Gandhi was unique among twentieth-century political leaders. He launched a non-violent resistance against British rule which became the inspiration for many other nations. Like a true Hindu he was in favour of accepting the good ideas found in all religions. Thus the Bhagavad Gita and the New Testament were his two favourite books.

9 Rites and ceremonies

The joyous spirit of Hinduism is most obvious in the festivals that take place all the year round. Hindus celebrate the change of seasons with as much gaiety as they do the stages of life such as birth and marriage. Even funerals and feasts in honour of the dead have a certain air of festivity.

The name-giving ceremony is an important event in any infant's life. The priest decides on an auspicious day on which a name is to be chosen for a child – this date has to fall before its first birthday. On the day of the name-giving ceremony, the child is fed its first spoonful of rice by its maternal uncle. With this symbolic gesture the child is formally weaned from its mother's milk and takes the first step towards adulthood.

The thread-giving ceremony (Upanayana) is another important ritual for a male child born into a Brahmin family. This is again a ritual gesture, it is meant to show that the time has arrived for the child to enter the second stage of life when he should dedicate himself to the life of scholarship.

This Hindu man is performing his midday prayers and offerings to the gods.

He is introduced to the secrets of the Vedas and to the Upanishads and formally relinquishes his ties with his 'natural' mother and father. His 'teacher' has given him the light of knowledge – he is 'born again'. For this reason Brahmins are often called the 'twice born' (Dvija). All women and non-Brahmins were barred from the knowledge of sacred texts – so they were never allowed to undergo Upanayana. Over the centuries, however, society has changed and so has the system of education. The right to universal education meant that men and women, Brahmin and non-Brahmin, now have equal access to the sacred Sanskrit texts, and some of the best-known scholars in Sanskrit these days are, in fact, women and non-Brahmins.

The most festive of all the rituals is of course the wedding

Left *A Hindu wedding. In the foreground you can see some of the food which will be offered to the gods as part of the ceremony.*

Right *This picture shows a Hindu bridegroom on his way to the ceremony.*

ceremony. Often this will last for three days with hundreds of friends and relations coming to join in the wedding feast. The bridegroom promises to cherish his bride and to protect her. The bride wears a gorgeous sari in bright colours, usually mostly red, and is bedecked in precious jewels. A Sehnai, which is a kind of Indian oboe, is played and the music reflects the mixed mood of the ceremony – joyous and hopeful for the couple's married life together and sad as the bride leaves her father's house for good. For when a Hindu girl marries she becomes a member of her father-in-law's family.

Hindus are cremated rather than buried when they die. The banks of the Ganges, which is the sacred river of the Hindus, is considered to be the ideal place for a cremation to

43

Above *On the banks of
the river Ganges families
come to burn their dead.*

take place. This is because Hindus believe that the water of
the Ganges absolves the body of earthly impurity and
ensures peace of the soul after death. When Hindus die in a
place far away from the Ganges, relations try at least to scat-
ter the ashes of their remains in the nearest river or the
ocean. The funeral ceremony is rather elaborate. The body is
placed on a funeral pyre, then the sacred fire is lit. The son
or sons of the deceased person pray for the peace and rest of
the departed ancestors in front of the sacred fire. Traditionally, daughters cannot perform this ceremony. That is one of
the reasons why it was considered essential to have a son.
For only the prayers of a son could ensure the peace of the
soul after death.

Right *This picture shows
some of the traditional
temple dancers.*

10 Festivals

Dates of festivals are always arranged by the Hindu calendar, which is different from the Gregorian calendar we follow in the West. 'Vaisakha' is the first month of the Hindu year and their New Year's Day falls somewhere in the first and second week of April, depending on the year. The beginning of each season is also celebrated as a festive occasion, and even the most religious of occasions assumes an air of carnival when the whole community is involved in the celebrations.

The most important of all religious festivals is possibly 'Dussera' or Durga Puja. This celebrates the victory of the great goddess Durga, who is the protector of good and the destroyer of evil. According to the Puranas, she is the daughter of the mountain Himalaya and is married to Shiva.

Right *This picture shows a street full of people during Holi. At this time people throw coloured powders at each other and even the strictest Hindu enjoys himself.*

Left *Diwali – the festival of lights.*

In popular tradition, this daughter of Himalaya comes back to earth for ten days to visit her father's folk, with four of her children – Lakshmi, the goddess of bounty, Sarasvati, the goddess of learning, Ganesha, the elephant-headed god of success, and Kartikeya, the general of the gods. An image of the goddess is made by the community. After ten days of festivity which also celebrates the success of the harvest, she departs and the whole community mourns as the image is immersed in the Ganges.

This ceremony is felt to be specially important because it reminds families of the temporary visits of married daughters to their parents' home. The daughter returns to her husband's home and there is another year's separation before the family is re-united. The women of each house kiss the

goddess goodbye as they would a dear daughter and ask her to come back again. This is an example of a strong personal bond between a god and her followers. A god comes to earth in the shape of a daughter – the joy of meeting and the pain of separation are just as essential a part of the festival as the rituals performed by the priest.

Diwali is another spectacular festival – often it is called 'the festival of lights'. It is held in late autumn when all the windows of houses are illuminated by lamps and candles. From a distance and in the darkness of night one can see hardly anything but these hundreds of glowing lights – a wonderful sight.

The festival of Holi takes place in spring. Hindus re-enact the playful mood of Radha and Krishna – the eternal lovers –

The holy city of Hardwar. Thousands of pilgrims bathe here to purify themselves.

by throwing coloured powders at each other. This is the day when traditional taboos are waived and even ladies from very strict Hindu families are allowed to be boisterous.

Another important festival is Ratha Yatra (Chariot Festival), when the famous image of Jagannatha (Krishna) at Puri in eastern India, takes a short trip in an impressive chariot. A Hindu can earn great religious merit by pulling the chariot and many Hindus eagerly take part in this procession.

11 Status of women

Hinduism is possibly the only religion in the world in which a god is often visualized as a woman. The earliest inhabitants of India worshipped the great mother goddess. From the ancient period onwards, the worshippers of Shiva considered his companion, Durga, the great goddess, to be as great as Shiva himself.

In spite of the importance of goddesses in the Hindu religion and mythology, women have in the past been rather unfairly treated by Hindu society. Until recently, Hindu girls were expected to marry someone of their parents' choice at an early age. Parents had to find large sums of money to obtain suitable husbands for their daughters. It was consi-

This illustration shows the ancient practice of 'sati,' where a widow would throw herself on her husband's funeral pyre.

*These women belong to
the lowest caste in India,
that of the Untouchables.*

dered a matter of deep shame to have an unmarried grown-up daughter in the family. Once married, a girl was expected to obey and follow not only her husband but all his people. In the case of an unhappy marriage, there was very little the girl could do. Even her own parents could do little to help her since a married woman was considered the property of the husband. According to Hindu tradition, a woman is never free. She is always dependent – in childhood on her father, in adulthood on her husband, in old age on her son. According to the old traditions, once she was widowed her life was very miserable. For, although a widower could marry without much difficulty, a widow was expected to lead a very harsh existence, never being allowed to re-marry, shaving her head, wearing no colour except white, and eating only simple vegetarian meals. Before the nineteenth century, good Hindu women were even encouraged to die on the funeral pyre of their husbands, a custom known as Sati (The Pure Woman). This rather gruesome practice was outlawed by the British Government in India with the help of reformers led by Ram Mohan Roy in 1829.

Attitudes have changed considerably, especially over the last few years. Hindu reform movements in the nineteenth century supported the cause of women's education and social improvement. Women graduated from universities and took up professional careers for the first time in the late nineteenth century. There are constant pressures even now from the more liberal members of society and from various women's organizations to give women equal rights and opportunities. As educational and economic opportunities increase, women become more successful in asserting their rights and breaking away from the traditions which favour men.

In spite of rapid changes the old values still play a dominant role in deciding a Hindu girl's duties in the family. Obedience and modesty are still considered essential virtues of a well-brought-up girl. At times, parental attitudes leads to conflict with girls of the younger generation, especially those who have lived all their lives in the West. Hindu girls want to have the freedom to lead their own lives and make their own decisions, like girls in the West. The most common cause of dispute is usually the arranged marriage. Even today most Hindu families expect to choose their daughter or son's partner. To an Indian boy or girl who has never lived in India, and who is used to the Western practice of choosing one's own husband or wife, this is a very unpopular custom which many are refusing to follow.

12 Hindus abroad

There are approximately 550 million Hindus in the world, most of them living in the Indian subcontinent, which includes the countries of Nepal and Sri Lanka. The influence of Hinduism is easily seen in the language, architecture and culture of a number of other countries in south-east Asia, but there is hardly any trace of Hinduism as a practising religion there, except in the island of Bali, in Indonesia.

Outside India, Hinduism is practised only by the communities that emigrated to other parts of the world from India. From the early nineteenth century, the British Government recruited labour in India for the rubber and sugar plantations in various parts of Africa and the West Indies. The British colonies in Africa also offered new opportunities to the trading communities in India, especially those from Gujerat. People emigrated in the hope of improving their standard of living, but they carried with them the religion and traditions of the country of their origin. Often these immigrant communities observed the rituals and taboos of their religion with even greater zest – being so far from home, they needed a sense of identity. Parents worried that the children would forget Hindu beliefs and traditions in an alien country. The caste system, arranged marriage, Hindu festivals – all these were strictly practised amongst the Hindus who emigrated.

The largest group of Hindus living abroad is in East Africa. The forefathers of most of them came from the Gujerat region of India. Gujeratis are traditionally traders and a large number of trading ventures in East Africa, until recently, were owned and run by Gujeratis. After many of the East African countries became independent in the mid-

*More and more young
people are refusing to
follow the old custom of
arranged marriage.*

twentieth century, people of Indian origin ('Asians' as they are called in Britain and Europe), were given the choice between British and African citizenship. Since most 'Asians' went to East Africa with the encouragement of the British government, a large number of them opted for British citizenship whilst continuing to live in Africa. After several generations in British East Africa, most 'Asians' there had developed stronger links with Britain than with India. This fact, along with the British citizenship granted them, made Britain their sole choice of refuge when they were expelled from East Africa by dictators such as Idi Amin of Uganda.

53

Most of the Hindus living in Britain at present are refugees from East Africa. Although a large number of them have never been to India, India is still very important to them because their religion and culture originated there.

During the 1950s and 1960s, some Hindus came to Britain as part of a post-war wave of immigrant labour from India. There was a shortage of labour during the post-war reconstruction period all over Europe, and immigrants from the countries of the newly founded Commonwealth provided the much needed labour in this country. However, out of the 750,000 people who emigrated from India and Pakistan, approximately 130,000 were Hindus. The majority of immigrants from the Indian subcontinent were Sikhs and Moslems.

The total number of Hindus living in Britain today is 300,000, making Hinduism an important religion in this country.

Left *Many 'Asians' were forced to leave Uganda by the dictator Idi Amin. Some settled in Britain, such as those shown in this picture.*

13 Hinduism and the West

Over the last twenty years a large number of people in the West have become interested in the principles of the Hindu religion. Young people especially feel disenchanted with the obsessive pursuit of material wealth by much of society. They feel that the desire to become rich and successful contribute to the pollution, ecological imbalance and tension of the present-day world. Disillusioned Westerners look for an alternative philosophy, to that of the materialistic West. The deep spiritual complexity of Hinduism, with its message of tolerance, love and frugality, makes it attractive to Westerners in their search for inner peace and tranquillity.

The most recent encounter with Hinduism in the West has been through Maharishi Mahesh Yogi, who preached the benefits of Transcendental Meditation (TM). TM is a special form of Yoga which offers the person who practises it relief from the tensions and pressures of modern living. Maharishi became a household name in the 1960s when thousands of young people, including famous film stars and pop idols such as the Beatles, flocked to his ashram in search of 'true' happiness. Although the first wave of enthusiasm has worn off, TM is still taught to a large number of Westerners through hundreds of centres in Europe and the United States.

The International Society of Krishna Consciousness is another example of the West's urge to find an alternative life-style in Hindu religion. The Hare Krishna people, with their chanting and robes, are a common sight these days, even in the most unlikely places, such as Oxford Street in London. Through devotion and love for Krishna, they give

The Maharishi Mahesh Yogi had many followers from the West, including the famous Beatles.

up all material comforts and personal possessions in order to awaken the consciousness of God within themselves.

The spiritual restlessness of many people in the Western world has made it possible for many imposters to come from India to make money by exploiting their young disciples. Hinduism is a religion which promises a personal bond between God and the believer. God's presence is always assured. It is not necessary to go to a church, mosque or a temple to discover God. To experience Brahman or God is in fact to wake up, as it were, from one long sleep of ignorance. Buddha, the founder of another religion in India which has

Tolerance, peace and kindness to others is the message that Hinduism wishes to teach. It is certainly one worth learning.

much in common with Hinduism, was once asked: 'Who are you? Are you a god?' 'No.' 'Are you an angel?' 'No.' 'who are you then?' He replied: 'I am the Buddha, the awakened one.' This is the essence of Hinduism – awakening the god in oneself. This is what attracts the Westerners to Hinduism.

Glossary

Asian immigrants People from countries such as Uganda who were forced to leave African states and come to Britain and other European countries.

Atman The Hindu word meaning the soul or spirit of an individual.

Aryans The original race from which European people are believed to have descended.

Brahmin The highest caste or group in India. This group provided the priests and leaders of ancient India.

Buddha A prince from northern India whose name was Sidhatta Gotama. He abandoned his life of luxury to discover the true meaning of life. He was the founder of the Buddhist religion.

Caste system A system where everyone was divided into separate classes. The caste a person was born into decided what job they could do and, in some cases, even where they could live.

Cult A group devoted to a particular deity or god.

Dhoti A long cloth, usually white, which is worn by Indian men. It is wrapped around the lower half of their body.

Gujerat A region in India where many of the people are involved in overseas trade. Many of the Asian immigrants were originally from this province.

Gandhi, Mahatma A nationalist leader whose aim was to bring about the independence of India through peaceful means. He was shot by a Hindu fanatic while he was campaigning for tolerance between Hindus and Moslems in India.

Hare Krishna A group or sect who believe in the importance of world peace. They are often to be seen in London and other large cities preaching their message.

Harijan The lowest caste in India. This group were also called the 'Untouchables'. They were the people who performed the most menial jobs, such as sweeping the streets and cleaning public lavatories.

Sanskrit The offical language of the Hindu religion. It is usually used only for religious purposes.

Sari The traditional dress of Indian women. It is a long piece of cloth, usually made of silk or cotton and often brightly coloured. It is wound around the body in a series of intricate folds.

Sufi mystics A group of Moslems who have a particular belief.

Transcendental meditation A traditional Hindu practice of relaxing the body and the mind by the repetition of a word or phrase.

Yoga Similar practice to meditation but the emphasis is on a series of physical exercises.

More books to read

Nahda's Family by M. Blakeley (A & C Black 1977)

The Many Faces of Religion by Dicks, Merrik (Sanders and Ginn 1973)

God of a Hundred Names by V. Gollancz and B. Green (Gollancz 1962)

World Religions and Beliefs by B. Evans (Macdonald Educational 1978)

Religions of the World by Sylvia Bates (Macdonald Educational 1979)

Index

Picture Acknowledgements

Alan Hutchinson Picture Library 8, 37, 38, 41, 44, 47, 53; Ann and Bury Peerless frontispiece, 7, 9, 11, 12 (both), 13, 15, 17, 18 (both), 19, 21, 22 (both), 24, 25, 26, 27, 28, 29, 30, 31, 33, 34, 35, 42, 43, 45, 46, 48, 49, 50, 58. All other pictures from Wayland Picture Library.